the guide to owning a
Canary

T.F.H. Publications, Inc.
One TFH Plaza
Third and Union Avenues
Neptune City, NJ 07753

This book has been published with the intent to provide accurate and authoritative information in regard to the subject matter within. While every precaution has been taken in preparation of this book, the publisher and author assume no responsibility for errors or omissions. Neither is any liability assumed for damages resulting from the use of the information herein.

ISBN 0-7938-2001-4

www.tfh.com

Contents

The canary crest is a mutation that has been known for at least 200 years.

Introduction

The canary, *Serinus canaria*, as we know it today, is nothing like its wild ancestor that was found on the Canary Islands in the Atlantic Ocean off the western coast of Africa by the Spaniards in 1496. The bird we know today sports an array of colors, shapes, and feather patterns that the original canary breeders would not even be able to recognize.

The wild canary is a mere 12.5 cm (4.92 in) in length. The male has a light yellow/green breast with a yellow/green throat and cheeks. The belly, rump, and sides of his neck are green. There is a green/gray streaking along the sides of the breast and flanks. The beak is a light horn color. The female shows much less yellow coloration and is grayer with an altogether duller coloration.

The breeding season of the wild canary begins in February with the male singing to attract his mate. The hen alone builds the nest that is made of grasses and fibers. She lays three to five eggs that are then incubated for 13 to 14 days.

Unlike the wild canaries originally found by the Spaniards on Canary Island, today's canaries come in a wide variety of colors and shapes.

Though canaries were once so expensive that only those of nobility could own them, today anyone can have one.

HISTORY

When the Canary Islands were conquered by the Spaniards in 1496, soldiers, sailors, and merchants all fell in love with these little songsters and brought many of them back to their homeland. The singing canary quickly gained popularity.

The cost of one of these gems rose so high that only the wealthy could afford them. Thus, the canary became a symbol of status and nobility.

Spanish monks took such a great interest in breeding canaries that they were able to conduct a lively trade. Not only were the canaries sold in Spain, but they were exported to Italy, France, and England. The Spanish monks wanted to preserve their fortune and therefore only male birds, not females, were sold. Most customers, however, only wanted male canaries because they sang and the females did not. The public wanted no part of breeding these birds, and it was therefore left to the monks.

It was very much different in Italy, however. No one knows for sure exactly how female canaries reached Italy, but it is generally believed that wild-caught birds came straight there on a trading vessel. Perhaps Spanish monks made a mistake and sexed a group of birds incorrectly, or perhaps a few females did sing. It is very rare but possible to have a female that attempts to sing; of course her voice is nothing of a song as the male's, but certain people consider this a song. In any case, by 1600 canaries were being bred in Italy too, and it was here that the first mutations occurred.

6

At the same time canaries also reached England. Toward the end of the 16th century Elizabeth I employed servants and court keepers specifically to care for and breed her birds. Thus, just as in Spain, canary keeping in England became fashionable among nobilty.

Canary breeding was not done on a large-scale basis until the common layman was able to purchase stock. The basic trend in breeding then was concerned with the birds' outward appearance, and there was very little interest in producing a bird for its song. It was generally believed that these little birds sang naturally, and it was not known that they could be taught to sing better.

When the Italian-bred canaries reached Germany, miners in Tyrol, an alpine region in West Austria and Northern Italy, saw that they had a chance to make a few extra dollars by breeding canaries. Actually, canary breeding proved to be more successful than their mining jobs, and with the mine industry declining, canary breeding became a primary means of support for most of these families.

New color mutations began to surface and yellows, variegated yellows, whites, and variegated whites became available. To these breeders, however, color was not important, it was the beautiful song the birds produced. Although their song was naturally beautiful, the Tyrolese breeders thought they could teach the young male canaries the beautiful song of the European Nightingale. Naturally successful, canary selling came to its peak in the 18th century.

Whether you are interested in an unusual breed or a common canary, obtaining the right bird should not be difficult.

The singing abilities of canaries captured the fancy of Europeans, and subsequent selective breeding resulted in Rollers, the preeminent singers.

The Hartz Mountain region had more in store for the little canary. It was the Tyrolean miners who brought the canary to the Hartz Mountains, and not only did they accompany them into the mines to keep the miners safe from too high levels of carbon dioxide, but they learned a new type of song from the rolling waterfalls that were above the mines. Hence, the Hartz Roller canary was born. Canary breeding here also flourished and it was from here that all of Europe and America obtained its stock.

BREEDING FOR SONG

Birds with the best songs were worth much more money and so breeders became busy with breeding to improve song. When birds of magnificent song were bred and their products did not sing as well,

breeders believed song was not a hereditary factor and that it needed to be taught and learned. It was then learned that heredity did play a vital role in how able a bird was to learn how to sing. Both heredity and teaching went into producing the best singers.

While the Germans were busy creating the ideal songster, other countries began producing birds of different shapes, forms, and colors. Different strains of birds came from England, primarily those of shape and form, and France and Holland produced canaries with frilled feathers.

The Hartz Roller set the standard for what all other songsters should be like—from them, other song canaries have come about. The Waterslager has a much more varied song and sings with his beak wide open compared to the closed bill of the Roller. He has a large repertoire and his song sounds more natural, uninhibited, and wild. The Spanish Timbrado has a song different from the other two, his song sounds like a tinkling little bell. The American Singer resembles the Hartz Roller in song; however, in this breed, song, color, and type are united.

What has not changed over the centuries is that people are attracted to the little canary for its beautiful song. It is for this reason that canaries are purchased as pets in the home.

Selecting the Right Canary

The best time of year to purchase your canary or canaries is from October through December. This is when they are, or should be, at their peak physical fitness. By purchasing your canary at this time you will be assured that he will be in his best condition. Older canaries have their breeding season behind them, have their molt completed, are rested up, and anxious to find a mate for the next season. Last year's chicks will be

Although personal preference plays a large part in choosing a canary, it is critical that you bring home a healthy bird.

Before making the commitment to owning a canary, it's important to understand that equipment—such as containers for food and bathing—will be required.

between seven and nine months old, may have gone through their first molt, will be in super feather, and be extremely lively. Either an older bird in top condition or a feisty young bird will be the best choice for a pet because they are displaying general good health. No one wants to start out in the bird fancy with a sickly bird that cannot even hold his head up. The birds you have to choose from should have a sturdy build for their type and not be overweight.

CHOOSING A BIRD

When selecting a canary as a singing companion in the home, there are several things that you should look for. A canary will live 10 to 12 years on average, and if you do not start off with healthy stock, this lifespan cannot be attained. Be sure that you are comfortable with the establishment that you have chosen to purchase your bird from. It should be clean, well stocked with birds as well as feed and accessories, and it should have a knowledgeable staff that is capable of answering all of your questions.

Stand back a few feet from the stock and observe for awhile. Be sure no birds are sitting fluffed up in the corner of the cage. This is a sign of illness, and in that case all of the stock would be infected. All birds within a cage should be sitting on a perch, have good, tight feathers, and clear eyes. These are the obvious things to look for. Once you have chosen a bird, take a closer look

Take time to carefully observe the birds you are considering. A healthy canary should have tight feathers and clear eyes.

Technically, only male canaries sing, so either ask the seller to identify the males or watch the birds to see which ones are actually singing.

at it to be sure the vent area is clear and not stained suggesting a recent problem. Be sure the bird has good weight to its body and that the breast bone is not protruding. There should be no missing feathers, and the bird's feet should have no excess scales or lumps. A bird with any of the above mentioned symptoms should be passed over.

All birds will sleep for short times periodically during the day, and any bird should awaken and tighten his feathers immediately when approached. A sick bird, however, will be very different compared to a healthy bird in his sleeping patterns.

Healthy birds sleep on one leg on a perch while sick ones use both legs and most likely will use the floor of the cage. Do not purchase a sick bird simply because you feel sorry for it,

you will be sorry in the long run if you do. Notify the seller that there is an ill bird in the cage, and choose a bird from another cage. The ill canary should immediately be removed by the seller and the others must be watched very closely.

If you are shopping for a singing companion in the home you should be advised that only the male canary sings. The female makes small little chirps that may mimic a song, but a male combines rolls and tours together to make a very pleasant sound. Upon looking at the birds, you will not be able to distinguish a male from a female. The seller may even have difficulty in doing so. This takes many years of experience and the birds must be in breeding condition to know for sure. You must trust the seller on this matter; however, be sure that a guarantee is given with the bird stating that it is a male and if it should not sing once you bring it home, you should be able to exchange it for one that does.

If the establishment allows, you may also stand back and wait for a male to begin singing. When a male canary is in breeding condition, he sings loud and strong to attract a mate. If there are other males present, they will all probably sing at the same time to compete against one another. Choose the bird with a song you find most attractive.

A singing companion in the home should be housed in his own cage. Do not feel sorry for him and try to pair him up with another bird. A male housed with a female will not sing. He sings to attract her, and if he already has her, there is no point in him wasting his energy. Two males cannot be housed together because they will fight during the breeding season. Your little singing companion will be best left alone with only you to please.

Canaries do not sing all year-round. They only sing during the breeding season and then they molt, usually during the summer months. Molting is much the same as a dog or cat shedding. All birds molt at least once a year, sometimes twice, depending on the conditions in your home. Over the course of three months your little canary will lose all of his feathers and regrow new ones. This is a gradual loss, however, and you should not notice any bare patches on the bird, only an abundance of feathers on the cage

Although females may occasionally present some warbling or mimicked notes, only male canaries engage in full singing.

THE GUIDE TO OWNING A CANARY

floor. Molting takes a lot out of a bird. The whole process uses much energy, and therefore a male canary stops singing during this time so that he does not exhaust himself.

You can help your canary get through his molt much quicker by providing him with a diet that is rich in oils and by keeping him at an appropriate temperature. (Appropriate meaning cool, but not drafty, and with high humidity.) If you keep your canary too dry, he will not grow his feathers in properly. They will be brittle and give the bird a shaggy appearance.

When choosing breeding birds, there are several things to look for. Naturally, they should be of good health. Look them over in the same manner as was described for the pet canary. If you are breeding for a specific color, you will have to trust the seller about the ancestry of the specific bird you choose. The same goes for those birds of a specific type. It is helpful to bring someone knowledgeable with you or you should read more specific books on this subject before you purchase your stock. Be sure that the breeding birds are young and really fit, otherwise they will not have the stamina to endure the entire breeding season.

No matter what type of canary you are looking for, it is imperative that it be healthy when you purchase it. Should the bird look ill at any time in the first week, immediately call the

You may be tempted to house canaries together. However, the best singing results from canaries that are housed separately.

seller and relay the symptoms. Watch the bird's droppings and make sure that it is eating properly from at least the second day on. Do not expect your new pet to eat for at least the first day due to the stress of moving.

QUARANTINE

If you own other birds, it is also a good idea to quarantine your new pet for at least 21 days. In this manner, should the new pet have any type of illness, it will show itself before you infect the rest of your stock. Never purchase a bird and place it immediately in with others, otherwise you are asking for trouble. Sometimes the stress of movement alone is enough to manifest an illness, and you would not want to have your remaining stock become ill because you failed to quarantine one bird.

Housing Your Canary

Cages and aviaries are the two basic types of housing used the world over for canaries. The difference between the two strictly lies among the needs of the owner.

Cages will be used by those intending to keep only one bird as a pet in the home or by those who wish to set up stock for breeding. There are many different sizes and styles of

The cage you provide for your canaries must be equipped with several perches, which provide resting spots as well as a means of exercise.

Many owners find that it's useful to have a traveling cage in addition to a regular cage. Both must have perches and food and water containers.

cages to be found in pet stores these days, and if you shop around you can easily find one that not only fits your budget but will accommodate your pet well and match the decor in your home.

CHOOSING A CAGE

The specifics you should look for in purchasing a cage for your pet canary are size, ease of cleaning, and sturdiness. The cage you choose should be wider than it is high. Canaries, like all birds, fly back and forth, not up and down, and need to exercise properly. It should be large enough so that the canary can achieve exercise from flying back and forth and not merely a hopping motion. Width, ideally, would be the same as the length. The cage should have feeders that are easy for the owner to reach and a pull-out tray on the bottom to facilitate daily cleaning.

The cage should also detach easily from its base for a very thorough cleaning at least once a month. The bars should be spaced close enough together so that the canary cannot get its head caught. It should be made of a durable plastic, as this proves easy to wipe clean and does not rust like metal.

A cage should be sturdy and able to hold up for many years without falling to pieces. You may have to pay a little more for a better quality cage, but in the long run you will have this cage for the entire life of your canary instead of having to purchase two or three lesser quality cages.

Cages can be purchased from your local pet shop, and it is best if you get this prior to picking up the bird so that you are ready for the arrival of your new little pet.

Like other birds, canaries need plenty of exercise and entertainment; swings and toys in a cage help provide both.

BREEDING CAGES

Breeding cages will be somewhat different than those used for housing pets. They too, however, will incorporate a few of the same basic guidelines. They should be spacious enough to house a pair of birds and their chicks comfortably, be easy to clean, and be sturdy.

Most breeding cages found on the market today are either all-wire or wood-backed with a wire cage front. Either type proves just as successful as the other, and it is truly a matter of personal preference which one you choose. Both cages prove just as easy to keep clean, the all-wire one can easily be wiped clean and the wood-backed type can be freshly painted anytime it becomes too dirty looking. Most breeding cages are available with wire partitions for the middle to

Several perches of slightly different sizes are required to keep your canary's feet from getting tired of gripping in the same position.

separate the male and female if spats become too violent. This usually happens when the female is still rearing a clutch of chicks and the male wants to go back to nest. The wire partition serves as a means that the male can still feed the chicks as well as the hen, yet cannot harm either.

Breeding cages are usually of the stackable type, which allow you to keep a number of these within one room without becoming overcrowded. They are relatively easy to clean and maintain, and prove to last a great number of years. These can be purchased from your local pet store.

AVIARIES

Aviaries are more sophisticated, and several considerations must be taken into account before one is erected. Naturally, an aviary can be an indoor unit; however, it is then most often referred to as an indoor flight. It is more the norm to refer to an outdoor flight as an aviary, and it is this that we will consider as such when speaking of it here. Before you purchase a unit to be constructed, or construct one yourself, check with your local zoning board about the proper permits and specifications that such a building must follow. Also, give word to your neighbors about what you are going to do so that they will not be upset. Not everyone finds the sight of an outdoor structure appealing, and not everyone enjoys the song of the

Birds love to take baths. You can purchase a birdbath that clips to the side of the cage.

canary. It is best to know this before you build the structure.

Be sure to purchase an aviary that is easy to maintain and that can withstand the elements of heat, snow, falling leaves, driving rains, and dropping branches before your expensive project turns into a pile of rubble. Ask your local pet shop dealer to recommend a reliable model.

Many bird keepers find it helpful to incorporate utilities such as electric or water services, and/or guttering to remove the rainwater, a drain in the center floor to facilitate cleaning, or shrubbery to make a very attractive unit.

There are several good books on the market that will help you get started, and this author advises that you talk to a few aviary-owning friends to see what advice they have to offer. Some of the best advice comes from aviary-owning fanciers that wish they originally incorporated other objects or utilities into their own structures.

No matter what style aviary you choose, there are several things that all should incorporate. If outdoors, the aviary should not be accessible to neighborhood cats, wildlife such as raccoons and foxes, or vermin such as rats. Mosquitoes, too, can pose a great threat to your birds; therefore, the proper screening should be on the outside so that none can enter. All aviaries should have a double-door access system. This type of system allows you to enter the aviary through one door, close it behind you, and then enter the actual flight. In this manner, no birds are able to escape.

Your birds may fare perfectly well in the wintertime in an outdoor aviary as long as they are accustomed to the cold weather from the late summer. There must also be a plastic covering placed around the structure so that the birds are protected from driving bitter cold winds.

ACCESSORIES

The type of fittings that you will need for your cage or aviary are basically the same. Perches and feed and water containers are needed. The perches should be made of real wood. Doweling can be purchased from a hardware store or natural branches from non-toxic trees can also be used. If you intend to use the natural branch, be sure that it is thoroughly disinfected with a suitable solvent.

Many owners prefer to add natural accessories such as twigs and branches to their canary's cage.

Perches are best if they are of varying widths, for this gives the birds' feet exercise and thicker branches will help to wear down the nails.

When a wooden perch appears to have become too soiled, it can be cleaned with a scraping of a knife and then a soaking in a disinfectant. If you feel you would rather purchase fresh, by all means do so. Remember that infections and illnesses can easily spread from one bird to another from soiled perches; birds rub their beaks on them and are constantly walking on them. It is easier to avoid infections and illnesses by cleaning the perches on a regular basis.

A variety of feed and water containers can be purchased from your local pet store. The type you decide upon will depend on your specific needs. There are basic considerations that will benefit all canaries, whether they be pet or aviary birds.

The first and most common mistake that keepers make is purchasing covered dishes to minimize the amount of seed spilled or wasted. Most canaries do not know how to eat out of such a dish. They can see the food but cannot get to it, and must therefore learn to do so. If owners are not aware of this, their canary can literally starve to death. Be sure that if you intend to use a covered dish of any type, you also place food on the floor of the cage or in a separate open container in addition to the dish until

THE GUIDE TO OWNING A CANARY

Though your canary may get along fine with other birds such as budgies, fighting may occur if more than one male bird is housed in a cage.

you see that your bird has been eating out of the covered dish. Gravity type feeders are another source of potential problems. They are wonderful in the sense that they supply your bird with fresh seed all the time, and that you do not have to feed the bird until the feeder runs low; however, they can become jammed without the bird keeper's knowledge. Should you choose to use this type of feeder, be sure to check it twice daily, making sure that the seed is flowing and is exposed for the canary to eat.

Many canaries enjoy rooting through their food bowls to find their favorite seed. This often creates quite a mess and much seed often falls on the floor. Canaries enjoy picking through what seed has fallen, and it may be easier for you to offer your pet its seed in an open container on the floor. In this fashion you do not have to worry about it becoming jammed as in the gravity feeder, nor do you have to worry that your bird is unable to find its food as in the covered dish type.

Water containers are rather simple. These can be of either the gravity type or open, but never covered. Covered dishes pose the problem of a canary attempting to take a bath within, and then becoming stuck and drowning. It is much safer to use the other types so that no unfortunate accidents occur. Be sure that the type of vessel you choose is easy to clean. Water containers must be cleaned on a daily basis so that bacteria does not build up.

Care and Feeding

All canaries, whether they are pets, aviary, or breeding birds, require the same basic care. Breeding birds will need extra attention regarding their food when they have chicks in the nest, and aviary birds will need extra amounts of foods containing fats to keep them warm during the winter.

SEEDS

A good canary seed mixture can be purchased from your local pet shop. This should contain oats, rape seed, and canary seed. Extra conditioning food and song food mixtures are advised to be fed to all types of canaries, and the amounts of these will vary according to the needs of the bird. Canaries should have a full seed container in front of them at all times. Be very careful to check this twice daily, making sure it is not filled

Because canaries have a high metabolism rate, they require a large amount of food. Be certain that your bird is supplied with food at all times.

Although a canary's main food is seed, greens and other fresh foods are fine dietary supplements.

get a certain amount of vitamins and minerals from their seed diet. It is not possible to control how much of any one seed a bird will eat. This is why such a large variety must be given. A wild canary will forage about and consume a variety of seeds, grasses, and vegetation, and thus will meet its daily nutritional needs. Pets in the home are dependent on their keepers to supply them with this variety that not only meets their dietary needs, but that does not bore them to consume it day in and day out. This is why additional foods such as spray millet and greens are so relished by our birds; they break up our birds' routine while providing other necessary components of the diet.

Breeding birds will require either soft food or rearing food in addition

with shells. It is very important that fresh seed always be available to your bird(s). Many keepers have passed over their bird's feeding dishes because they appeared to be full, when in fact they only contained the empty husks of seeds.

If you find that your bird has a particular liking of one seed for another, you may purchase this seed separately and feed it in addition to the mixture. Never feed a favored item as a sole diet. Birds need to get their vitamins, fats, proteins, and carbohydrates from a varied diet. No one seed can supply all this for your bird.

To meet their dietary needs, a good mixture must supply your canary with all of the constituents. They must also

When a male and female canary have paired off, they may feed each other as part of their courtship.

to their basic seed mix. This type of food is designed to provide the chicks with the proper amounts of proteins and carbohydrates to ensure proper growth. Without rearing foods, the parent birds are forced to work harder to consume large quantities of seed, digest them part way, and then regurgitate them back to their chicks. Rearing foods are of a softer composition, will digest quicker, and will fill up the chicks faster than seed. You can purchase rearing foods from your local pet shop, or feed some other type of soft food that you have composed. Hard-boiled eggs, scrambled eggs, pastas, rices, and other high protein/carbohydrate items will provide the chicks with the essentials.

VEGETABLES

Green, leafy vegetables of all sorts are very much liked by all birds. Be certain that greens collected from the yard, such as dandelion, kale, or lettuces, are free from pesticides, insecticides, car exhaust fumes, fertilizers, and other hazards prior to offering them to your birds. Likewise, any greens that are purchased from the grocery store should be thoroughly washed to ensure against the same.

TREATS

An additional treat that nearly every type of bird enjoys is sprouted seeds. This can easily be done by taking a small amount of seeds such as rape seed, placing them in a jar and covering them with water. Allow this

When keeping several birds, be certain you provide enough food for everyone. More aggressive birds may intimidate the other birds.

to soak overnight. Drain the water from them 24 hours later, rinse, and place them in the same jar but inside a darkened cupboard. After another 24 hours, the seeds should have shoots coming from them. After a final rinse these can be fed to your birds. Only fresh seeds will sprout. Old seed will not. This is also a good way to periodically check to see that your supplier is carrying only quality seed.

NUTRITIONAL REQUIREMENTS

Carbohydrates supply your bird with energy. Being such a small and active bird, the canary requires quite a bit of this. The highest quantities of this can be found in oats, canary seed, millet seeds and biscuit meal. Nearly all seeds, even those of an oily nature, contain a large proportion of carbohydrates, and most seed-eating birds, like the canary, are unlikely to suffer from a deficiency.

Fats are necessary in the canary's diet as a concentrated source of energy. They are necessary for proper skin condition and feather growth. Common sources are rape seed, thistle, hemp, and egg yolk. It is especially important to feed these seeds prior to a bird's molt to ensure proper feather growth.

Protein is just as important in your canary's diet as it is in your own. Protein is composed of approximately 20 nutritionally important amino acids

Canaries require plenty of fresh water, which should be changed once a day—and twice a day during the summer.

that are body building foods essential for growth. Particularly important during the breeding season, females require proteins for egg production, and the young birds need them for essential growth. Of course, during molting season, the replacement of feathers is entirely dependent on protein. Most seeds contain a good amount of protein, but during the critical times other sources may be added, such as eggs, milk, whole meal and oatmeal, to name a few.

Life, either human or bird, would not be possible without minerals. Calcium, phosphorus, magnesium, potassium, sodium, chlorine, and the trace elements manganese, iron, copper, zinc, iodine, molybdenum and selenium all have different functions and are all vital to life.

Minerals can be attained through foods and additional supplements available from your local pet store.

Vitamins are also needed by birds in relatively small quantities. If any vitamins are lacking, certain deficiency diseases may become apparent. The best safeguard against vitamin deficiency is a balanced diet that contains green vegetables, egg yolk, milk, yeast, and wheat germ oil, as well as a basic seed mixture.

WATER

Without water, no creature would be able to sustain life. It is a solvent and

With the proper diet and care, your canary should thrive for many years as your companion.

acts as a transport medium for nutrients and products of metabolism, via the bloodstream, to the cells of the body. It also removes waste materials through the kidneys.

Be sure to supply your canary with a good source of water, preferably spring water. City or tap water can contain harmful amounts of chemicals that may eventually cause your canary to become sick and die.

It is important that food and water be changed on a daily basis. Should your canary enjoy bathing, offer a separate dish for this purpose on the floor of the cage in the early morning so that the bird has all day to dry off. Birds that bathe in the evening tend to catch chills quicker and fall ill. In addition to the seed, morning is the time to offer any green or soft food. These must be removed by midday because they quickly spoil and if consumed in this state your bird could fall ill rather than benefit.

OTHER NEEDS

The floor of the cage should be lined with a suitable paper material. Brown paper bags, newspaper, or paper toweling work best. On top of the paper, a small handful of gravel containing charcoal and oyster shell can be placed so that the canary can go to this and pick through it as needed. Gravel is needed by small birds for digestion purposes. Being that they do not have teeth, canaries will consume bits of gravel and store it in their gizzard. As they eat seed, it will pass through the gizzard and be pulverized, making digestion easier. Change the papers on the bottom of the cage at least once a week.

A cuttlebone should be placed somewhere in the bird's cage so that it is accessible all the time. Your canary will use this as it is needed, just be sure it is there for him. Most cuttlebone have two sides—one that is soft and should face the bird so it can get to it, and the other side, a hard shell, should face away from the bird. Cuttlebones are good until only the hard outer shell is remaining. After this, discard it and replace it with a new one. Some birds seem to never use it, which simply means they are receiving all their minerals and salts from their diet. Other birds require more, and consequently seem to devour this within days.

Keep your canary out of a draft, out of direct sunlight, and keep a small night light on during the evening so

A varied diet complete with the necessary vitamins and minerals will keep your bird in shape.

that your bird can see should something frighten it. Most birds panic so much in the middle of the night that they injure themselves by hitting against the sides of the cage because they cannot see.

Breeding

There comes a time in one's bird-keeping hobby that just "keeping" these birds is not enough. The love one develops for the birds he/she keeps transpires into a passion that must not be permitted to die out, and therefore the only natural solution is to breed them.

When one then pursues breeding these wonderful creatures, what really occurs is the all-out effort to breed for a "better" bird, whether this be in song or in type. Only the best specimens are used to develop this ultimate bird, and through very careful selections the correct genetic trans-

For most bird keepers, breeding is carefully coordinated to produce the best possible birds.

THE GUIDE TO OWNING A CANARY

missions are made and the species continues to improve.

Canaries are very popular birds to breed for several reasons: they do not require much space, and they produce chicks annually, allowing the breeder to see his results the very same year; in this way he can make the necessary changes to abolish the lesser characteristics.

Canaries are very prolific birds, laying three to five eggs per clutch, with an incubation period of 14 days. The chicks fledge in approximately five weeks, with the hen feeding them for another week or two until they are completely able to feed themselves. The pair then quickly goes back to nest. Sometimes the hen will have already begun a second clutch before the first brood of chicks fledge.

Although the breeding of canaries seems simple, there are several things that the breeder must do to be sure that all runs smoothly for the pair. To begin, after the selection of the best male and the best female to be paired has been made, the birds must be properly conditioned. The breeding season for canaries is normally from February through June (this can be made longer with the addition of artificial light simulating longer days). Conditioning birds for breeding must begin in the cooler autumn months, September and October are best. By conditioning, what is meant is to really prepare both the male and female for

Wire mesh or plastic nests are easy to disinfect and wash after each breeding season; wicker must be discarded.

the five months of work that lies ahead. A pair must be physically fit, not overweight, exhibit good overall health, be active, and be free of all parasites before breeding is even attempted. The best way to condition birds is to set them up in very large cages so that they receive plenty of exercise and supply them with the right combination diet of carbohydrate, fat, and protein to maintain a good weight. When the birds are properly conditioned, you may then move on to pairing the two birds together in the hopes of breeding success.

It is important that one realizes that a male and a female canary cannot simply be added together in a cage and expected to successfully breed and raise young. The pair should be placed in two separate cages or in a double breeding style cage that has a

Because female canaries build their own nest, it's important to provide yours with the appropriate nesting materials.

wire partition in the middle, with the male on one side and the female on the other. Supply the female with an open type nest, nesting material, canary seed mix and canary rearing food, and plenty of calcium supplements to ensure her health and vigor. The male should be supplied with both types of food and calcium supplements as well. As soon as the male begins singing to the hen, and she is building the nest, the partition can be removed and the two will begin to mate.

The nest that is constructed by the hen will be quite beautiful, and in some instances the male will pull the entire thing apart immediately after she has finished. She must then begin again. The second nest tends to be constructed even tighter and is woven with whatever materials are provided in the hopes that her mate will not destroy this one too.

EGGS

Eggs will be laid approximately one week after the first mating. The birds will continue to mate until the entire clutch is laid. Sometimes the pair will mate several times within one day. When the hen begins to spend much time on the nest, you should expect to find the first egg. Remove this egg and replace it with an artificial one purchased from your local pet store or specialty breeder. Set the real egg in a safe place where it cannot break; however, be sure that it stays at room temperature. Canaries lay their eggs every other day, so expect to find the second egg and remove it too, replacing it with another artificial or "dummy" egg. Do the same with the third egg. On the day the fourth egg is laid, replace all the dummy eggs with real eggs and then mark down this date. You should expect to find several chicks hatching in 14 days.

The reason the eggs are removed and replaced with artificial ones is to ensure that they will all hatch on or about the same day. A canary in captivity begins to brood her nest the very same day she lays her first egg. This means that incubation begins that very same day. If the eggs are not removed, then in a clutch of five or six eggs, the first chick will be eight to ten days old by the time the last chick hatches—a considerable size difference. Wild canaries do not begin incubating their eggs until the last one is laid. The difference in the behaviors of the captive and wild canary is probably due to the domesticity of the birds.

NUTRITIONAL NEEDS

Rearing food is supplied prior to the eggs even being laid to accustom the birds to eating this. Canaries, and most birds in general, will not feed something to their chicks that they are not familiar with. Do not be alarmed if they do not seem to eat any of this, at least they will be familiar with its presence in the cage prior to the chicks' hatching. A good rearing food can be purchased from your local pet store, or you can feed a number of different soft foods to your birds. Cooked eggs, either scrambled or hard-boiled, soft corn, boiled potatoes, cooked rice or any other nutritious, soft food will be suitable to feed to a breeding pair of birds. The pair will

benefit from this and the chicks will grow at a rapid rate.

Calcium is very important for the hen canary. Her body will use this supplement in the formation of the eggs. Without the proper amount of calcium an egg will not develop the proper hard outer shell, and the hen will have much trouble in trying to pass this. This is called being egg bound. Sometimes she strains so much in attempting to pass such an egg that it breaks inside her, causing her to die from peritonitis poisoning. A cuttlefish bone supplied in the cage is a good way to ensure your female is receiving enough calcium, and crushed oyster shell added to the grit is another way.

Because canary chicks grow at such a rapid rate, they require constant feeding for the first three weeks.

If both of these are supplied, you should have little to worry about regarding egg binding unless your hen was not in proper breeding condition before this.

AFTER HATCHING

As a breeder, your job is not finished after the eggs have hatched. True, both the male and female will care for their young. They will feed them and keep them warm; however, the soft food must be supplied for them constantly, and because this sours easily, it must be changed at least twice a day. Never leave food in the cage all day to spoil. If you have plans that do not allow you to change the soft food, it is better that you do not supply it. Birds can easily perish from eating spoiled food and this is no way to begin breeding attempts.

LEG BANDS

At approximately five to seven days of a chick's life a leg band may be placed on it for identification purposes. Banding canaries is the breeder's choice, and unless the bird is to become a show bird, there is no legislation that requires a canary to carry this form of identification. Leg bands can be purchased from your local pet store or from specialty avicultural stores. They usually carry a breeder's initials and year so that there is no question as to a bird's age. There are specific bands required by national

societies for show purposes, and if you think your birds will be involved in the exhibition side of the hobby at any time in their life, you should check with the society on its requirements before you band your birds.

Banding is a relatively simple process by which a coded band can be slipped over a chick's toes and onto the leg without any hazards. The correct size band must be attained. A band that is too small would constrict the leg as the chick grows, and this could cause circulation to stop. Likewise, a band that is too large could either fall off or easily catch on even the most minor protrusion in the cage. Again, it is solely the breeder's choice to band his birds, and he should be sure to obtain the correct size so that no unfortunate accidents occur.

WATCH THE MALE

It is also the job of the breeder to ensure that all the chicks are being fed and are in no way being harmed by an overzealous male that wants to begin breeding his hen again. When the chicks first hatch, they are quite helpless and will not even be able to lift their heads. This will quickly change, though, as the growth rate of birds is quite spectacular. Within four weeks the chicks will have most of their feathers and will begin hopping out of the nest. It is your job to simply pick them up and place them back. This will only last for a few days before the chicks then decide that they do not care how much you try to keep them in their nest, they would rather be out of it.

Should the male become too harsh toward his chicks, replace the wire partition in the cage, leaving the male alone on one side while the female and chicks are on the other. In this way he can easily assist feeding the chicks through the wire. The chicks will begin eating on their own between the fourth and fifth week of life and should not be removed from the cage until you are absolutely sure that they can maintain a good body weight. When they are completely weaned, you may remove them and again allow the male and female to rear another clutch in the same manner as you did the first.

If your male behaved himself and never bullied the hen or the chicks, it is quite possible that he resumed mating his hen before the chicks were weaned and she may have even begun to lay eggs again. This is fine, providing the chicks do not interfere with the incubation process. That is, they should not be permitted to sit in the nest with the hen while she has a clutch of eggs. Remember to remove and replace the real eggs with artificial ones as was done with the first clutch to ensure the

New breeders should decide whether song or color will be their goal in breeding birds.

hatching date of all will be relatively the same.

Do not allow your pair of canaries to raise more than two clutches of chicks per year. Any more than this is simply being greedy and really proves to be too much of a strain on the pair, especially the hen. When the second set of chicks has weaned and has been removed from the cage, separate the male from the female and allow them both to rest. It should be the beginning of molting season, which also will take much of their energy, and so no added stress of breeding needs to be placed on the pair. Wait again until next season.

Molting

Molting is the process by which a bird gradually loses each feather on its body and regrows a new one. All birds

The molting process, which is typically completed in three to five months, usually takes place during warmer weather.

molt, just like all dogs and cats shed. A bird will molt at least once a year in its wild environment; however, in the home it is more likely that two molts will occur. It requires a lot of energy for a bird to regrow a completely formed feather. Therefore the molting season is never during a bird's breeding period, and male birds cease singing during this time. It is the bird owner's responsibility to see to it that the bird is placed under the best possible conditions to develop new plumage. This also includes seeing to it that the bird receives a proper diet.

For canaries, the molting season normally occurs after the breeding season during the warmer weather conditions. Usually this extends from late June to the beginning of October. It should not take any individual bird the entire three months to complete its molt. If it

Molting places a tremendous demand on a bird's metabolism; it's therefore important to provide a nutritious diet during this time.

does, then something is amiss with the bird's health.

Many keepers are unaware of the proper conditions for a canary to endure a quick and successful molt. Canaries always remain healthiest in cool and constant, but not drafty, temperatures, with a high amount of moisture in the air. You must not allow your canary's skin to dry out, otherwise the molt will be never ending and the bird's feathers will not grow in correctly. Unfortunately, many of us have forced hot air heating systems and inefficient amounts of humidity in our homes.

FEATHERS

A bird's feathers have two major functions: they act as protection against the elements or other birds, and certain feathers are specifically designed for flight. The protection feathers that cover the body are called contour feathers, and the flight feathers are called primary and secondary flights. The molting process follows a definite ordered pattern. It begins with the feathers on the wings and then gradually moves up throughout the entire body to finish up on the neck and head. The new feathers grow in the same spot that the old ones were located and a feather receives its nutrients from the bloodstream through a small opening at its base. Therefore, new feathers are filled with blood. Should your bird break a new feather while it is growing in, it will receive blood directly from the blood stream and continue to bleed until the feather is pulled out. Once the entire feather is pulled the bleeding immediately stops. A new feather will regrow in four to six weeks.

Although molting strains a bird's system and requires the bird to put energy towards this, it does not make the canary look sickly or act lethargic in any way. This is a perfectly natural system that all birds go through and there is no need to treat your pet as if it is terminally ill throughout this time. The proper rules of hygiene are especially important during this time. If we always treat our birds the way we should, then no additional attention will be needed during the molt.

A regular bath is always appreciated by canaries. Most enjoy their bath temperature with a bit of a chill to it. Always offer your bird a bath early in the day and be sure that there is no draft. By offering the bath early, you give the bird the entire day to dry off and to preen each feather so that it looks its best. Never give your bird a bath too close to nighttime. This would cause the bird to go to sleep

Remember that color-fed varieties of canaries should be fed coloring agents before molting begins.

before it was completely dry and could bring on a chill.

Molting can be compared to new hair growing in on humans; it reaches a stage where it becomes itchy, and bathing and cleaning bring relief. Bathing also helps to loosen old feathers, therefore losing them faster and regrowing new ones quicker.

COLOR FEEDING

Should your canary be a color-fed individual (fed additional supplements to either alter a bird's natural color or enhance it), then it is vital that this be given prior to the onset of the molt. The supplements must be within the bloodstream well in advance of any new feathers growing in. The aim of color feeding is to produce as deep and rich a color as possible, whether this be the bird's natural color or an artificial one. The most readily accepted fashion of color feeding is via the bird's soft food. It is simple to incorporate the supplement directly into the mixture and therefore have a good idea of exactly how much the bird has consumed by noting exactly what is remaining at changing time. If the supplement is placed in the water, it is not always known that the bird consumed as much as is missing from the container. The bird could have taken a bath or could have tipped the dish over, leaving its keeper guessing whether his bird actually drank any of it.

One of the best ways to prevent illness or help your bird through its molt is to follow proper hygiene and care procedures every day.

To attain coloring it is best to feed the canary the color food daily, throughout the entire season. In this manner, you can be assured that it is always in the bird's system, and should your bird go into an unexpected molt, you are assured it will be the proper color.

There are a few "picky eaters" that do not take readily to color food, but these birds can usually be tempted by adding honey or other sweetness to the mixture.

EXERCISE

The proper amount of exercise is also imperative during the molt. The bird's system must remain strong during this time, and the only way to achieve this is to be sure the bird has a large enough cage to fly back and forth in. Aviaries are perfect for this, but the single canary owner does not need to erect an aviary to satisfy the bird's needs.

As mentioned earlier, if proper hygiene and care are always adhered to, no special adjustments will have to be made to help your bird through its molt. A good healthy molt will get your bird into its finest condition and it will be ready for the breeding or show season faster than expected.

Health Care

Preventative measures are always your best defense against illness or disease invading your stock of canaries. Whether you own one bird or a collection of birds, there are certain basic rules that should always

Good hygiene results in good health. Get in the habit of cleaning your bird's cage and accessories on a regular, if not daily, basis.

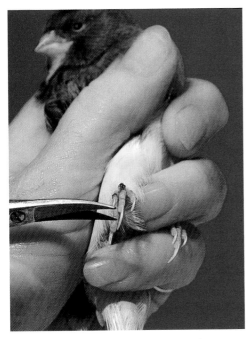

When it becomes necessary to trim your canary's claws, be careful not to cut into the blood vessel.

be adhered to. By following these simple measures, it will be very difficult for your stock to become ill.

BASIC HYGIENE

Always start off with healthy stock. A bird that is ill or has recently been ill should never be brought into a home. Movement only stresses a bird's system further and could immediately cause a relapse. Although a recently recovered bird may now appear healthy, it has a weakened system and should not be put through a change in environment, diet, or way of living. Avoid any bird that has had a recent illness.

Practice good hygiene with all of your stock. Never let up on this rule by thinking that you can make up for it

the next day. The next day is often too late. Good hygiene refers to the condition of the bird's cage, accessories, surroundings, and food. The bird's cage should always be clean. It does not have to be done on a daily basis unless you find that your pet is quite messy. Try to keep the floor of the cage as free of debris as possible. Your canary will, of course, drop its feces here; however, he will also go down to the floor to pick up seeds that have fallen to the ground and to consume gravel. It is perfectly natural for birds to do this, and this should not be denied. It is recommended that the floor of the cage be cleaned at least once per week, more if your pet is incredibly dirty. All of the accessories within the cage should be kept clean at all times.

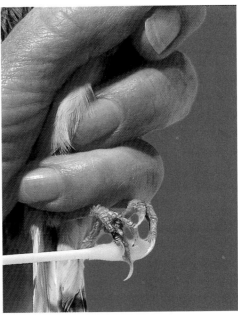

Clean feet are a must. Droppings and food remnants can stick to a canary's feet and produce inflammation.

Canaries kept in cages that are too small are often the victims of obesity. Proper diet and exercise will keep your bird in top shape.

This includes all feeders and water containers as well as all perches. Food and water containers must be cleaned on a daily basis, and perches should be cleaned and freed from debris and fecal matter at least once per week. Many birds fall ill from having these simple tasks ignored by their keepers. The area surrounding the bird's cage must also be kept clean. This is one area that many keepers fail to observe. However, the area surrounding the bird's cage must be kept as clean as the bird's cage itself. Keepers must see to it that their pets are in clean, airy, and draftproof living conditions at all times to ensure the best health for their pets. The food one gives to his or her birds should always be fresh and fed in proper quantities; it should also be of the proper nutrient content.

IF YOUR BIRD IS ILL

Your canary is dependent on you to recognize when it is ill. Our birds are not able to tell us when they are feeling ill, and we must be aware enough of their daily behavior to know when something is abnormal. Certain things to look for are a lack of interest in food or eating in general, loose or watery droppings, a change in the amount of energy that is being expended, difficulty breathing, and sitting fluffed up either on its perch or on the floor of the cage. As soon as any of these symptoms are noticed, it is imperative that they be acted upon as quickly as possible. Being such tiny birds, canaries can quickly lose weight and perish. If you are unable to contact an avian veterinarian, the best thing to do is to heat the bird's cage to approximately 85-90°F. Attempting to keep warm will use most of the energy the bird has left, and with having the heat supplied for it, the canary does not have to try to keep itself warm. Contact your avian veterinarian, relay the bird's symptoms, and get some medication for your pet. It is valuable to relay your bird's past history to the vet as well as any abnormal behavior the bird has recently displayed. This will help the veterinarian make a more accurate diagnosis. Follow the vet's instructions and do not stop treatment just because your canary "looks normal" again. Be sure the bird is completely healthy again before ceasing its medication.

The last and most important guideline to healthy stock is to apply the correct remedy for a specific illness. Do not try to play veterinarian; you may do more harm than good. There are so many diseases that have the same symptoms, but very few have the same remedies, you may falsely medicate a bird and actually be more detrimental to it in the long run. Unless you are absolutely positive, do not treat a bird without a veterinarian's approval.

While it is not possible to say that your birds will never fall ill if all of the above guidelines are followed, you can be assured that it is highly unlikely that they will.

Every bird keeper should also stick to a quarantine policy. A new bird should never be introduced to other birds without first having it carefully watched for several weeks. An illness may not show itself right away, and if you were to immediately introduce a new bird with your old stock, you could contaminate the whole bunch. It is much safer to keep the birds separate and to be certain that no problems will arise before adding the new bird.

Another rule of thumb is to never transfer a bird to an unsterilized cage. Even if you are sure the bird you are putting into the cage is healthy, you cannot be so sure about the last bird who occupied the cage. Everything in the cage should be disinfected: perches, feeders, waterers, any and all toys, cage bottom and all cage wiring. This will simply ensure that your bird is not beginning its life with you under infectious conditions.

COMMON AILMENTS

The most common types of illness that may strike your bird fall into two categories, respiratory and digestive. Respiratory diseases may range from a cold or chill to asthma and pneumonia.

As soon as a bird shows signs of illness it should be relocated to a cage by itself to keep others from becoming affected.

In all cases, the symptoms are the same—heavy, labored breathing often accompanied by wheezing. The respiratory tract becomes inflamed and the nature of this inflammation differs only in severity and location. Quite often, respiratory diseases are caused by bad housing conditions— damp, drafts, fluctuating temperatures, and inadequate ventilation.

Other infections are known and may be brought about by either fungi or parasites. In these cases, in addition to the difficulty in breathing, the bird will also sneeze or snort so as to release an obstruction from his nasal or throat passage. Parasites that occasionally make their way into the trachea are known as "tapeworms." This parasite is easily passed from one bird to the next, so it is therefore critical that the infected victim be removed as soon as possible. You must contact your veterinarian immediately for a safe remedy.

The digestive diseases that can affect your bird are usually constipation, diarrhea, enteritis, and indigestion. In all of these cases the lining of the digestive tract is inflamed and the bird exhibits sleepiness, fluffed feathers, and other obvious signs of suffering. Diseases of this nature can quickly lead to malnutrition and death because the bird is unable to assimilate its food properly.

Many times, digestive disorders are caused by contaminated foods or unwashed greenfood. Warmth usually cures the sufferer within a 24-hour

Too many fruits or greens can cause diarrhea, a problem that can become serious if not treated promptly.

A healthy canary will be a lively and active creature.

period. If your bird shows no improvement or appears worse, contact your veterinarian for a remedy.

There are, of course, other illnesses that are not associated with respiratory or digestive disorders, and these should be brought to the attention of your veterinarian immediately—physical accidents, slipped claws, and continuous molt are a few of the reasons to inform your vet.

Prompt action is essential when dealing with disease. Upon the first sign that something is amiss the bird should be isolated. There should be no question as to whether or not a bird should be removed from the remaining stock. Even if you only suspect that a bird might be ill, it is reason enough to remove it to a separate "hospital" cage.

HOSPITAL CAGES

A hospital cage is one that restricts a bird's movement and helps to cure an ailing bird of its illness. The cage should possess only a perch placed low and open faced seed and water containers on the floor. It should be solid on three sides with only the front made of wire. A heat source should be easily attached or already incorporated. This heat alone aids an ill bird tremendously as the bird therefore does not need to expend any extra energy to keep warm. A cage of this type should be ready-made and available should an emergency arise. You do not want to waste precious time preparing such a structure should your bird become ill. Immediately after a bird is removed from this, sterilize the entire cage and its contents, so that it is ready for the next time it may be needed.

PARASITES

Parasites that frequently infect birds do not usually cause a serious problem unless left untreated. Two types of parasites are usually found: the red mite and body lice.

The red mite is actually gray in coloration and appears red to the eye because it has been feeding on the host, your bird, and is filled with blood. These mites only come to feed on the bird at night. If you suspect your bird has mites you can place a white cloth over the cage at night and before sunrise the next day shine a bright light on the cloth. The red mites will be visible, It is not difficult to rid your stock of these creatures, however. They like to hide in the tiniest cracks and crevices of a cage and these should be thoroughly treated as well.

Body lice are gray insects that spend their entire life cycle on the bird. Unlike the red mite, body lice feed on skin and feathers. They prove to be quite annoying to the bird, and this is made quite evident by the amount of pecking and scratching the bird does to its plumage. If the bird is examined and the feathers are blown away from the body, some of these creatures can be seen trying to make their escape under the soft downy feathers. To rid your pet of these, the bird itself, not the cage, must be treated. The most common method is to dust the birds with an over-the-counter insecticidal powder. This treatment should be carried out again ten days later to ensure that any eggs that may have hatched are also gone.

There are many detailed books that can further inform you of diseases and treatments. These are filled with the latest methods of treatment available for the ailing bird.

Coloration

It is a common belief among those not familiar with the canary fancy that the canary is only available in a plain yellow color or its wild green coloration known as "self green." The truth of the matter is that between the clear yellow and the green are many other colors. Variegated, whites, reds, and dilutions of these, as well as buffs and frostings are all commonly found and well established. This chapter will briefly touch on each of these.

The food that your bird eats has a lot to do with its feather condition and coloration. The pigments that give color to a bird's feathers are derived from the food and deposited in the feathers at molting time. These pigments are yellow, black, brown, and red.

Naturally occurring pigments that are soluble in fats are known as lipochromes. They are what gives the canary his yellow coloring. Especially found in greenfoods, certain seeds, and egg yolk, these pigments deposit themselves fairly evenly throughout the feathering. The lipochrome is the ground color from which all other colors may or may not overlay.

Melanins are the dark pigments of birds. These are formed by proteins in

Breeding for color did not become a popular and established trend until the early 1900s.

Reports of white canaries go back as far as the 1600s, not long after the arrival of pure yellow canaries.

the bird's diet. Unlike lipochromes, melanins are by no means distributed evenly throughout the body. These mainly deposit themselves on the wing, tail, and central body feathers. Variegation is the term used by fanciers to describe the condition in which the dark pigments of the canary's plumage are confined to certain parts of the body while others remain pigmented with the lipochrome, or in this case, yellow.

VARIEGATED BIRDS

When speaking of variegated birds, several terms are used: clear, ticked, variegated, foul, and self. Clear refers to a bird that displays no dark pigments in its feathering at all. Clear birds are found in all light colors, yellows, whites, and reds.

The term ticked refers to a single area of dark feathers on a bird's body, wings, or tail. On the wings and tail this area may not consist of more than three feathers, otherwise it is considered a single dark mark.

A true variegated bird is one in which light and dark areas are exhibited irregularly on its body. A bird that is said to be lightly variegated displays less than half of its plumage as dark, and heavily variegated birds exhibit more than half of their plumage as dark. The amount to which a bird will be variegated cannot be bred for nor predicted. The most desirable variegated birds are those that display a symmetrical patterning.

A foul marked bird is the ticked bird's counterpart. As where the ticked bird displays only a single area of dark feathers, the foul bird displays only a single area of light feathers. This too can be anywhere on the body, wing, or tail and may not be more than three feathers on wing and tail.

A self-colored bird is one that has no light feathering at all, the clear

Features such as crests can be a factor in breeding canaries—whether you are breeding for color or for song.

bird's counterpart. No light pigments exist anywhere on the bird's body.

COLORATION

Birds that are referred to as "buff" lack lipochrome pigment in the very end of their feathers and therefore display a thin edging of white on the end of each feather. This is also referred to as frosting. In addition to this frosting, this type of bird does not seem to be so intense in its ground color as those that are not frosted. Dark pigmented birds display the buff as a grayish or silvery edging on their feathers. The frosted birds show their white edgings on the tips of their feathers. For the most part, the frosted birds are better in type than non-frosted birds. The feathers of these birds are usually more compact and therefore thickly distributed over the body.

The white variety of canaries either hide their lipochromes or do not have any, and therefore are lacking the yellow color. They are capable of displaying melanins and variegation patterns just as other colored canaries.

The dilute, otherwise known as agate canary, can best be described as a bird that displays a reduction in the melanin pigments of its plumage. The dilute seems to have been produced from an ordinary mating of green to green that resulted in a pale, ash-gray hen. Because it is rather pale the dilute has never had a large following.

The most popular of the canary colors

Red-factor canaries, bred by pairing a red-hooded siskin and a canary, have a wide range of red shading.

is the red-factor. This color canary did not happen by accident, however; it was deliberately bred for. Through many experimental breedings it finally came about when a red-hooded siskin and a canary were crossbred. This not only created fertile young, but young who carried the red gene and who could continue to pass it on to their offspring. This did not happen with one simple breeding, but took many years of patient work as well as back and cross breeding.

The coloration of the red-factor bird ranges from pale orange to very bright red. To intensify the red coloring, the red-factor may be fed color food prior to its molt so that it can be distributed into the bird's feathers as they are formed.

There are many color foods on the market that advertise themselves as able to change the color of any bird to red; however, this is only true if the bird carries the red gene. It is wise to feed such foodstuffs to your bird all year round so that its color comes in evenly rather than spotty.

Type Canaries

LIZARD

The Lizard canary is usually classified with the type canaries, although it does not possess an unusual shape nor hold itself in an unusual posture. Its

The Lizard canary's scaly plumage markings, from which the bird gets its name, make this canary unique.

distinctive feature is the unique coloration of its feathers. The Lizard canary's feathers are marked in a scaly pattern, reminding one of a lizard's markings, hence the basis for the breed's name.

The origin of the Lizard is not known for sure; however, it is believed to have arrived in Great Britain in the 16th century, and as most canary breeds, it nearly became extinct during the Second World War. If it were not for two very enthusiastic canary breeders, A.W. Smith and Robert H. Yates, who formed the Lizard Canary Association of Great Britain, the breed would have met a tragic fate. From the stocks of these two men, they began to propagate the breed again— improving on type and quality all the while.

The scaly markings of this bird's plumage are referred to as spangles

A good Border canary will possess a small, rounded head and a well-rounded, yet elegant, body.

on the upper parts and rowings on the lower parts of the canary. The rowings contain less melanin than the spangles and are therefore less evident. The spangles are a very important characteristic of the Lizard canary, in addition to the bird's cap. The cap must conform to the ideal size as dictated by the standard. The cap may be clear, broken, or patched. It is not uncommon, however, for a bird with particularly good spangling but a poorer cap to win at an exhibition over a bird with a clear cap and not so definite spangling.

BORDER FANCY

The Border Fancy canary is probably the best known type canary in most countries except for Germany. It is an old breed that was originally known as the Cumberland Fancy, named so for the area in which it originated; however, since this lay on the border between England and Scotland, it was agreed to refer to it as the Border Fancy to avoid dispute.

During the craze of the larger type canaries—Yorkshires, Norwich, and their like—breeders wished to have a smaller type canary. By breeding small Norwich with Harz Rollers, Lizard canaries, and London Fancies, the small Border Fancy came about. Its petiteness and neat appearance instantly made it very popular. It was, and still is, a wonderful bird for novice breeders because it does not have any of the characteristics or odd postures that are so hard to breed for in other type canaries. Its most wonderful advantage is its eagerness to breed. The Border Fancy is available in all colors except for red.

Like other canary varieties, the Norwich can be bred crested, with an assortment of color variations.

The Norwich's increase in popularity began in the mid-1900s and continues today.

NORWICH

There are several theories surrounding the origin of the Norwich canary, of which no real truth can be adhered. Some authors believe that during the 16th century, Flemish weavers who were trying to escape Spanish persecution brought them to England, especially Norwich county, and there they became established. Another theory suggests that these birds developed from Lizard canaries, London canaries, and simple ordinary canaries. In either case, these canaries were further developed in eastern England and adopted their name from the breeding center, Norwich.

Norwich canaries of one hundred years ago, although rounded in shape, were much lighter and slimmer than those we are familiar with today. At exhibitions, these birds were only outnumbered by Border Fancies, and the only characteristic that was important was a strong plumage color. Breeders then began to focus on the size of these birds. The very large Lancashire canaries and soft-feathered canaries were crossed in with the Norwich. This led to a devastating outcome. While it did result in a larger bird with very full plumage, it also resulted in birds with feathers that were too soft, so soft that they could not penetrate through the bird's skin and this created cysts. This tragedy nearly exterminated the breed within a relatively short time span.

During the 1950s an English breeder then began a strict selection of the "best" Norwich and crossed them with Border Fancies. This helped dramatically to return the bird to its special type and to its good health. A new standard was then implemented into the breed. The Norwich's plumage was to be soft, long, and full, but not shaggy. The bird was to be free of lumps and was to measure between 15 and 16 cm, no greater. Today the Norwich is a very popular bird the world over, especially in Britain.

CREST

The Crest canary is a breed with a large, circular crest on the top of its head. It is known that the Crest canary has been in existence since 1750 and has always commanded a higher price than other canary breeds. This is still true today. Just as the Norwich experienced a setback, so did the Crest. Breeders again were trying to "improve" the crest and wanted larger birds with bigger crests. This relentless breeding led to cysts in the skin of the breed and the breed's tendency towards obesity became increasingly obvious. The birds gradually lost their desire to breed, or perhaps they couldn't because they were too overweight and too ill. Only some countries have taken action to save the Crest canary and have strict breeding rules in the hopes that they can improve the breed.

Crested birds must be paired with non-crested birds in order to ensure young. Two crested birds paired together produces a lethal gene causing the young to die either before or soon after hatching.

LANCASHIRE

The largest canary breed, the Lancashire canary, has a length of 19 to 23 cm. This breed also has a crested form, known as a "Coppy." The non-crested form is referred to as a "Plainhead." As its name suggests, this breed originated in the county of Lancashire; however, no one knows exactly when this breed came about. It was well-known over two hundred years ago, and it is assumed to have been bred from the "Old Dutch" canary, except for the crest. The Lancashire was, of course, used in the development of other large breeds, especially the Yorkshire, which is so very famous today. This breed's numbers were also diminished because of feather cysts, and at the beginning

The Lancashire, a large canary used to develop other large breeds, can be found as a "Coppy," or crested, and as a "Plainhead," or non-crested.

The Gloster Fancy, one of the more popular canaries, is a small, roundish, lively, and compact bird.

of this century the breed was nearly extinct. Since about 1950, it has been bred in Great Britain with some success in increasing its numbers; however, outside of this country it is still virtually unseen.

Almost all of the birds of this breed are pure yellow; occasionally a pure white bird is seen. Melanin birds, variegated, and red-factor birds do not yet exist in this breed.

GLOSTER FANCY

The Gloster Fancy is another extremely popular type canary. It is small, roundish, lively, and bold. The Gloster is available in two types, the "corona," or crested, and the "consort," non-crested.

Developed in the 1920s in Gloucestershire, England, this breed was developed from the Crest, Norwich, Harz Roller, and Border Fancy canaries. It is amazing that a bird of such a dainty size, not exceeding 12 cm, can gain in popularity so quickly, especially during a time when sizable birds were in demand.

The Gloster Fancy is available in all colors except red, and two pairings should be avoided at all costs: never pair two crested birds together, and never pair two dominant white birds. Both pairings would result in the chicks dying close to hatching or just after, and so should be avoided. Otherwise, Glosters are very easy to breed and are quite prolific. This adds to their popularity and is why they can be purchased at a relatively low price.

YORKSHIRE

Developed from other large canary breeds, the Yorkshire canary is a very

The crest of a Gloster should be circular and even in form. The bill and the eyes should be clearly visible.

elegant and large type canary. Originating in 1870 at a time when the breeding goal was a smaller and more slender bird than the Lancashire, the Yorkie soon became the craze. It was said that around the turn of the century, the ideal Yorkshire had such slender shoulders and an erect carriage that it could easily pass through a wedding ring. The desire for larger type birds began again, however, and the Yorkshire began to gain in size. It attained a length of 17 to 19 cm and has remained there since. It is among the largest of the type canaries, and its erect posture and slender appearance make it an exquisite sight to behold.

Pure colored birds with very slight markings are most commonly available, and birds with extensive dark variegations are becoming more common all the time. Greens, browns, and blues are also known, and red-factor birds are available, but will not be as large as the other colors.

BELGIAN

The Belgian canary is an old breed that had much influence on the breeding of other canary varieties, notably the Yorkshire and Scotch Fancy. Very high prices were paid for this breed as it was an outstanding show bird and known as the "king" of the canary world.

Like most breeds of the time, the Belgian, too, suffered the effects of the First World War. The breed nearly

Yorkshire Canaries, like this yellow variegated green cock, should ideally not exceed 12 cm.

became extinct and has never fully recovered to this day. Some enthusiasts who worked hard in preserving the breed only faulted again during the Second World War.

Many fanciers thought the Belgian was a deformed bird, but its peculiar appearance turned out to be the trademark of the breed. The main characteristics of the breed are therefore shape and position, and it was the fact that it could assume this position on command in a show cage that made it so popular. It is often referred to as hump-backed.

The Belgian is a large bird of at least seven inches with a small head in proportion to its body. Its body is long and tapered with a straight back and closely braced wings. The famous show stance for the Belgian shows the line of the bird's back completely perpendicular to the perch. The head of the bird is depressed into its body with its beak pointing directly toward the bottom of the cage. This position must be held for several seconds so that the bird may be evaluated by a judge.

SCOTCH FANCY

Formerly referred to as the Glasgow Don, the Scotch Fancy originated in Glasgow, Scotland. Its odd shape gives it its popularity. The outer contour of its body forms part of a circle, thus leading to its other name, "bird o' circle." This was a very popular breed in Scotland and England until the beginning of the 20th century. Its numbers then dwindled almost to the point of

The Parisian Frill, one of the largest canary varieties, experiences some difficulty in breeding.

extinction. Recently, breeders in Great Britain, other mainland European countries, and even Germany propagated the breed again, and today Scotch Fancies can be seen at all major exhibitions.

The Scotch Fancy's resemblance to the Belgian canary is no accident. Because the Belgian is older than the Scotch, it is probably safe to say that the Scotch was developed with the Belgian's help.

When the Scotch Fancy goes into position, its nicely arched head-back-tail line becomes very evident. The bird extends its head forward and holds itself upright, with its legs fairly steep. The breast should not protrude, but should appear flat. The Scotch Fancy should adopt this posture long and often during exhibitions.

The Scotch Fancy is easily recognized by the arched line from its head to its back to its tail.

Most commonly seen in yellow, the Scotch Fancy is also available in green, variegated, white, blue, brown, and Isabele.

PARISIAN FRILL

The Parisian Frill was, in its early days, the largest canary breed of all. It was, and to some still is, the most impressive breed because of its abundant frills. The definite origin of this breed is unattainable. It is believed, however, that by the 17th century, the frill already existed in Paris.

During the breed's early existence the frills encompassed the entire body of the bird. They also gave the bird a different look, for some of the frills were in the small head feathers above the bird's eyes and appeared to be bushy eyebrows. Other frills gave the bird the appearance of wearing a cap, yet the wing feathers were always straight so as not to impair the bird's flight. Even the toenails of this breed grew with a curve, adding to the bird's appeal.

The Parisian Frill has always been a popular breed, and today its popularity seems to be increasing everywhere. Unfortunately, with such a large and odd-feathered breed, certain difficulties arise in breeding. Because of their shape and feathering, specialization is needed more with them than almost any other breed. Much inbreeding is

There is a wide variety of species and color patterns of canaries to choose from. Consider the characteristics of different canaries before making a selection.

Whichever canary you choose, you are sure to gain a loyal, long-lived companion.

THE GUIDE TO OWNING A CANARY

Those interested in breeding frilled canaries should begin with Northern Dutch Frills, as they are reliable and zealous breeders.

necessary to maintain this breed's characteristics, and because the birds are so closely related, individuals are usually blind in one eye or both. Also, the frills of some of these birds tend to be absent on one side or the feathers do not grow properly.

Being such a large breed, the Parisian Frill often has trouble making proper contact during mating, and if this is successful, it then has difficulty in incubating the eggs properly. Its long legs inhibit it from sitting tight on the eggs and many eggs are wasted because of this. Of course, there are some birds that not only mate, but manage to raise their birds without difficulty. It has become common practice for breeders to foster out the eggs of this breed to other reliable breeds to ensure the proper rearing of the chicks.

DUTCH FRILL

Although one may believe this to be a smaller version of the Parisian Frill, the Dutch Frill differs from its larger counterpart in its feathering. As it is much less densely feathered than the Parisian, it is the frilling of this breed that is of great importance. It is a very alert breed that shows itself well.

GIBBER ITALICUS

Created by Italian fanciers, the Gibber Italicus or Italian Humpback Frill is an offshoot of another frilled breed, probably the Dutch Frill. Combined with the frilled feathering, the Gibber also has a position in the show cage similar to the Belgian and Scotch Fancy. It is a small bird of slight form and only available in yellow varieties.

Song Varieties

Fanciers are first attracted by the beautiful song of the canary. It is, after all, the reason the bird was imported to Europe from the Canary Islands in the first place. The canary's song as we know it today is far different than that of its wild ancestor. It has been bred for, taught, and modified, time and time again. Several different variations exist; specifically the Roller, the Waterslager, Spanish Timbrado, and American Singer. In this chapter we will briefly look into each type of song.

The Hartz Roller is not only the best known song canary, but it is probably the oldest known as well. The color and type of these birds was not important to the early keepers of this bird, however, it was the quality of song that mattered. Yellow, green, and variegated birds did predominate, and later it became thought by the public that only these colored birds were good singers. Today, many people still believe this to be true. The fact of the matter is, however, that canaries come in a wide array of colors all with the ability to have a magnificent song and with many variations to the song. It was no easy task for breeders to combine the canary's magnificent song with the beautiful colors, but for the most part the bird world can find the best of both nowadays. For those keepers who only wish to keep a single songster as a house pet, a very wide array of birds with the combination of color and song are available to choose from. It truly comes down to a matter of personal preference.

HARTZ ROLLER

The Hartz Roller set the standard by which all other songsters followed. The "Roller," as it has come to be called, is no longer only found in Germany, however; it is available and bred widely in many other countries, including the United States.

The song of a Hartz Roller is very different from that of a color or type canary. The Roller's song consists of four passages known as tours: the hollow roll, bass, flute, and hollow bell. There are also three additional tours that very few birds are able to master: gluck, schockel, and water roll.

The hollow roll is the tour from which the Roller derives its name, it is also the easiest of the tours to detect. Bass is the deepest tour the canary is trained to deliver. The flute adds great richness to the canary's song. It is very accentuated and is often at the end of a delivery. Most mating calls of birds are flute notes, often soft and often before the start of tours. The fourth basic tour of the Roller is the hollow bell, it is slower than the roll and bass and is easily distinguishable as separate. It is a deep, perfect, hollow bell that many breeders have dedicated themselves to producing.

The supplementary tours, however difficult, are desirable because they can expand a bird's repertoire and therefore make a more interesting song. When learned incorrectly, however, they can reduce the quality of the song. Years of experience are needed to become truly familiar with canary song and to recognize differences within. If you are interested in this aspect of the hobby, it is worth

Song varieties can vary from bird to bird; take time to select the right songster for you.

visiting a number of shows and talking to judges. It truly takes a trained ear to choose a winner from among the best.

Song canaries are judged differently than type canaries. They are exhibited in teams of four with each bird housed in its own cage. They are placed in front of the judges and must deliver their song within 30 minutes. It does not matter how long the song of the bird is delivered, but the quality and blending of the tours is what matters. Each bird can earn up to 90 points.

WATERSLAGER

Germany was not the only country to breed song canaries. In Belgium, breeders wanted a song canary all their own, and approximately around the same time as the Roller originated, the Waterslager was born. Much loved in

It was the canary's song, not its color, that originally attracted fanciers. Today, singers can be found in an array of colors.

detract from the beauty of the bird's song, not improve it.

This interesting breed of song canary has greatly improved the fancy. The popularity of these little songsters seems to continually be on the uprise. The only limiting factor of this variety is the bird's color; the Waterslager can only be found with yellow coloration. If you are someone who wishes a bird of fancier color, the Waterslager is not for you; however, if you are looking for a very versatile song bird, look no further.

AMERICAN SINGER

Cultivated in the US, the American Singer resembles the Roller canary. In fact, the American Singer originated from crossing Border Fancy canaries with Hartz Rollers. They are bred in various colors such as yellow, green, gray-blue, cinnamon, white, and fawn. The red-factor has also been introduced; however, a solid strain has yet been developed. A few more years are still needed by breeders.

The song of the American Singer resembles that of a warbler, it is neither too loud, too soft, nor is it too harsh in its tone. It has been described as an outstanding, free, harmonious song that is very pleasing to the ear and has much variety.

The American Singer is not known much outside of its homeland, but is very highly recommended as both a good singer and pet.

its area of origin as well as Holland, Italy, France, South Africa, North America, and South America, the Waterslager has a large following.

To describe it, the Waterslager is quite similar in shape to the Roller, though slightly larger and stockier. The true difference between the Roller and the Waterslager lies in the song. The Waterslager's voice is very versatile and has been compared to that of the nightingale. While the Hartz Roller sings its entire song with its bill closed, the Waterslager sings all 17 of its tours with an open bill. Although no bird has been known to master all these tours, it is easy to see that the Waterslager's voice is more varied than that of the Roller with its four main tours.

It must be noted that these two varieties of song canaries may never be cross bred. Doing so would only

Taming and Training

Canaries have a natural fear of movement, especially overhead, and do not like to be handled. They are naturally nervous and flighty birds that should be kept away from all hasty movements. They do not display affection towards their owners as do other birds, and tend to be somewhat removed.

Although not advisable because of the accidents that can occur, canaries can be let out of their cage to fly free and trained to fly back to it on their own. After about two weeks in its new environment, the bird is reasonably familiar with the room it is in. It can then be let out of its cage. Do not chase the bird out, however,

The first step of training is to allow your canary to feel comfortable in its surroundings and with you.

Keeping canaries separately increases their training ability. Training will help you form a close, loving bond with your bird.

just open the door. Sooner or later the bird will notice the opening. Food should not be placed outside of the cage. When the bird is tired or hungry it will find its way back into its cage and then the door may be closed. A bird that is allowed the exercise of flying around the house will require more food than one that does not exit its cage.

Keeping canaries separately increases their training ability. Taming and training a canary is nearly impossible with more than one bird in a cage. It should be kept separately with no disturbances. It is important that all of the bird's attention is focused on you and not on other birds. Two male canaries must never be kept in the same cage. Not only will the birds sing a lot less and not be trained, they may also attack one another. Birds that are housed together, however, do not want to be bothered with people.

With patience you can teach your canary to perch on your hand. To do so, remove the perch and position the cage so it is at eye level. Insert a pencil or finger into the cage and gently try to induce the bird to perch. Doing this everyday will familiarize the bird with you and it will become more trustful. A canary can gradually be trained to eat seeds from your hand. This can be accomplished by holding your hand in the cage with seeds in the palm for a few minutes each day until the canary begins to take seeds from this. Keep in mind that birds must be trained separately at first and then in pairs and trios so that they can be company for each other.

Exhibition

In keeping canaries, the general order of progression is normally as follows: first, one keeps one canary, then two, perhaps several; second, one moves to breeding his birds; ultimately, the birds are exhibited at shows. Bird showing or exhibiting ensures a breeder that his efforts are not wasted and that he is capable of producing birds that are equal to or better than his colleagues. Only through side-by-side competition can one truly see the difference. Naturally, when conversing with a fellow bird keeper, we envision specimens that in actuality may be poorer or better than what they really are.

Bird shows also provide a social outlet for breeders. It is here that one can speak to other fanciers, newcomers to the hobby, and those interested in just getting started. You can also discuss issues, exchange information, discuss new methods of breeding or rearing, and new items that have entered the market with each other. A bird exhibition acts as a shop window to the entire fancy. Advertisers from all over usually set up samples of their new products as well as hand out information and pamphlets about other products they have to offer. Bird breeders, too, get in on the action, and it is here that they can sell or advertise their surplus stock.

Many bird keepers who have been successful at breeding canaries choose to show off their birds at shows and exhibits.

The Frilled Canaries, with their elegant and impressive plumage, make fine candidates for showing.

There are many shows that you can attend, and most are held annually. These can be on a small, large, and even international basis. Society shows are small shows in which only members of that society participate. Open shows permit all comers and not merely members of a specific society or club. Specialty society shows are huge. These usually are open to all those interested; however, they are sponsored by a particular society.

Most canary exhibitions require that the style cage one exhibits his stock in be of a standard type. In this manner the judging can be assured to be the most fair to other competitors. Different breeds do have different standard cages, and you should check with the society or club that is hosting the show as to what style they wish you to use.

Birds do not instinctively show themselves to their best advantage, and therefore training is necessary. In front of a judge your canary must be steady and hold itself in the correct posture. It in no way can cower in a corner and hide. Training a bird for a show usually begins soon after the young chicks are weaned. A breeder usually places a show cage adjacent to the potential show bird's cage and keeps the door open. Eventually, curiosity gives in and the youngster hops into the show cage on its own. The breeder will leave the two cages in this manner for awhile allowing the bird to hop back and forth. After a week or so of this, the youngster is closed into the show cage for a short time, and this period progressively gets longer until the bird is able to spend a couple of days within. This is equal to the amount of time that a bird would have to spend within the cage during a show. After the bird is steady within this for the maximum time, it is vital that you train it to remain steady no matter what approaches the cage. Try to have as many different people enter your home and peer into the cage wearing all manners of clothing, hats, and accessories, including eyeglasses. To train a bird to stand in the proper showing position, that special stance that shows the bird's best qualities to the judge, requires time and a great deal of patience. The bird must stand in the same position for the time period that the judge is watching it. A judge will not waste his time on an unsteady bird. The Border Fancy canary and the Yorkshire must show themselves well because position and carriage are allocated a definite value in the scale of points.

To enter a show you must obtain a schedule of the classes provided. Local shows usually dispatch these immediately to all members of the club. For a schedule of an open show, you must write to the secretary of the hosting club and request one. Many times the open shows are advertised in newspapers and it is from here that you can obtain the secretary's name and address.

Bird shows have two categories under which an exhibitor may show, novice and champion. The bird is not the one who receives the title, but it is the exhibitor, unlike dog shows. A novice exhibitor is anyone who has never won a first prize in a champion class or three first prizes in a novice class at any open show. Separate classes are provided for champion and novice exhibitors.

The bird's feathers should be clean. Try to avoid hand washing the bird. If you do have to do so, be certain that you give the bird an entire week to get its feathers back to their original sheen. Washing removes the natural oils from the bird's feathers. It is not until the bird preens itself that these oils are replaced. Preening is the process by which a bird runs its beak through each and every feather, occasionally going to its oil gland located at the base of its back, and distributes oil over all of these so that they are soft and glossy. The whole preening process can take a bird several days until it is satisfied with its appearance.

Upon arriving at the show you will receive labels to place on your show cages from the secretary of the club. Be sure the show cage is touched up with fresh paint and that it too is in its very best condition.

The floor covering of the show cage should be in accordance with the society rules. Some will permit a coating of seed, others prefer that it be plain paper. All rules for the show should be fully understood prior to the show so that you can inquire about anything you do not understand.

Canary judging takes place on the basis of visual comparison, except in the case of the Roller canary, who is judged on his song. All judging is done without spectators. When judging is complete and all awards have been made, the judge arranges the birds in order of merit according to the standard. It is at this time that the birds may be viewed by the public.

Index

Photo Credits

Dr. Herbert Axelrod, P. Demko, Isabelle Francais, Michael Gilroy, Eric Ilasenko, Horst Mayer, Ron and Val Moat, Robert Pearcy, and Mervin F. Roberts